For Wyatt and Whelan

www.milove.org

ISBN: 978-0-578-39981-2

Illustrations by Heather Workman & Kathleen Andrews

Good Day, Harbor Country!

Regan Keating

Illustrated by Heather Workman & Kathleen Andrews

Good day, Great Lake Michigan!
Good morning, sandy dunes.

Good morning, golf cart riders,
listening to tunes.

Greetings to the exercisers,

as they run, bike and walk.

Cruise over to the deli for
coffee and some talk.

"Helloooooooo," canopy trail,

way up there in the trees.

Can you see the kayaks below?
Does your lookout sway with the breeze?

Good afternoon, Warren Dunes State Park.

Climbers reach the summit.

Then racing to the water,
into the waves they plummet!

Heading north on Red Arrow Highway,

places to explore.

Pick fruit or find a treasure, inside an antique store.

IDA RED

Golden Delicious

SIDEWALK SALE

Fri • Sat •

9 am

Hi, beautiful fall colors,

trees of orange, yellow and red.

Hello pumpkins, hello corn mazes,

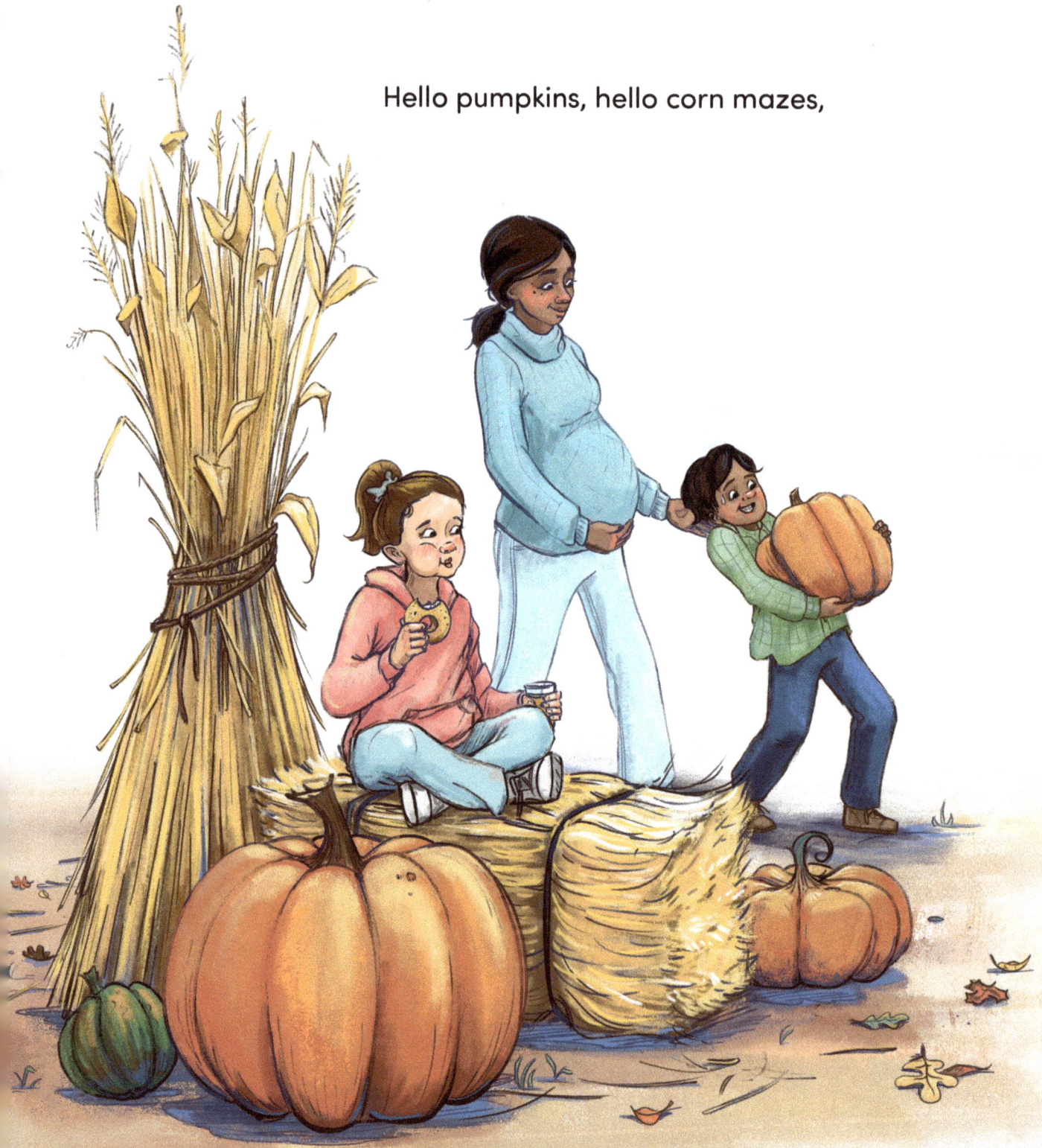

hello farm goats to be fed.

Good evening, music in the park.
Children dance and play.

Parents and grand folks listen.
They hum along and sway.

Hike on up the snowy hill as the sky turns dark.

Good night to all the sledders, at Oselka Park.

Good night, blue waves, reaching up to the setting sun.

Thank you, Harbor Country. Today was so much fun!

"Until next time," Harbor Country.

www.ingramcontent.com/pod-product-compliance
Lightning Source LLC
Chambersburg PA
CBHW040251100426
42811CB00011B/1221